Delhi Agra & Jaipur

Delhi Agra & Jaipur

Text

Biraj Bose

Lustre Press

Delhi ◊ Banares ◊ Agra ◊ Jaipur ◊ The Netherlands

elhi, Agra and Jaipur—they represent and unravel the mystique that is India. New Delhi, the elegant capital with its wide roads, sprawling gardens and stately buildings, stands on the site of eight historical cities built by the visionary rulers through the centuries. Agra, the capital of the glorious Mughal emperors, harbours the incomparable Taj Mahal, the exquisite marble monument that attracts millions of visitors every year. Jaipur is the enigmatic pink city of the Maharajas, the city of pomp and splendour, of colour and festivity, of a rich and regal past that continues into the present.

This is the golden triangle—a visit to which is essential to get a glimpse of India's rich past. Though the cities are very different

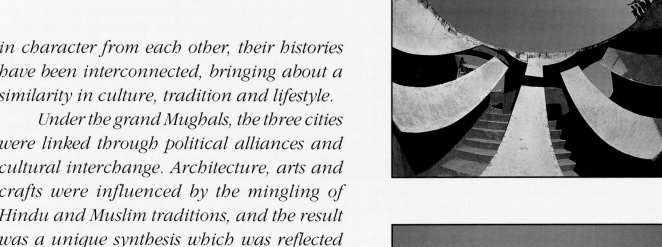

in character from each other, their histories have been interconnected, bringing about a similarity in culture, tradition and lifestyle.

Under the grand Mughals, the three cities were linked through political alliances and cultural interchange. Architecture, arts and crafts were influenced by the mingling of Hindu and Muslim traditions, and the result was a unique synthesis which was reflected in the literary life and performing arts of the cities. With the establishment of British India, these three centres were absorbed within the fold of the empire, and their colourful histories took a new turn into the future. Located at a motorable distance from each other, these cities are easily accessible and form a must for every tourist.

5

Centre : *Royal splendour amidst the rugged Aravalli Hills. A Kalbelia dancer entertains the visitors.*
Clockwise : *The devout at prayer at Jama Masjid, Delhi.*
Wholesale market for dried fruit at Khari Baoli, Chandni Chowk.
Kite making is a traditional craft and the Kite festivals held in January inspire the creation of colourful and imaginative kites.
Retainers enjoying a moment of leisure at the City Palace, Jaipur.
Rajasthani women rarely allow themselves to be photographed.
Dedicated to the Sufi Saint Nizamuddin Aulia is the dargah (shrine) in New Delhi.
Images of Hindu gods and goddesses.
The Sikhs in Delhi form a large part of the population.

Preceding pages 6-7: The Jantar Mantar at Delhi was built in 1724 by Sawai Jai Singh II of Jaipur to study the movements of the heavenly bodies. Pages 8-9: The Taj Mahal, the unsurpassed monument to love, was built by Emperor Shah Jahan for his beloved queen Mumtaz Mahal. Pages 10-11: In 1727, Sawai Jai Singh decided to leave Amber to build a capital in the plains—the city of Jaipur. Following pages 14-15: The Samode haveli is now a hotel where the tourist can experience living like a Maharaja. The ceiling and walls are covered with frescoes. A folk dancer entertains the visitors. Page 16: The Diwan-e-khas at Fatehpur Sikri, built by Emperor Akbar, where he met courtiers and intellectuals. Here he met Hindus, Muslims and Jesuits and propounded a new religion based on tolerance and understanding—the Din-e-illahi.
Page 17: In contrast to the rugged exterior of the Amber Fort, the entrance—Ganesh Pol is exquisitely carved and painted with frescoes and leads to more luxurious apartments inside.

Delhi
A city of contrasts

Delhi presents a vast panorama of fascinating yet conflicting images. It is a city where forts, tombs and ruins share the skyline with high-rise buildings and stately homes. The wide tree-lined avenues of New Delhi give way to the crowded narrow lanes of Old Delhi—and along with this change comes a diametrically different culture and lifestyle. The presence of contrasts is a historical legacy of the city and the differences go far beyond the apparent.

Delhi is a metropolitan city in the true sense of the word. It has for centuries attracted rulers, invaders, businessmen, builders, poets, painters and intellectuals from many parts of the world. Today's Delhi encloses many older cities—it's stone walls have seen many empires rise and fall. Delhi's poets have described its unrivalled glory and mourned the number of times it has been razed to the ground by merciless invaders. Due to its strategic position in the north, Delhi has been the site of a capital for eight different empires dating back to the fabled town of Indraprastha.

Indraprastha was founded by the Pandavas on the banks of the Yamuna. Archaeological excavations near the Purana Qila in Delhi have revealed several objects dating back to 1000 B.C., which are similar to the objects found in other places in India associated with the Kauravas and Pandavas. Urban Delhi, however, dates back to the second century B.C. when it was a part of the vast Mauryan Empire of Emperor Ashoka. It did not acquire the status of a capital until the establishment of Rajput Kingdoms by the Tomars and the Chauhans in the eleventh and twelfth centuries. The Tomars ruled from Haryana and had first settled at Surajkund where they built a large amphitheatre reservoir. Surajkund today is a popular spot and the site for an annual crafts fair in the beginning of February. Artisans and craftspersons from all over the country find a market for their traditional embroidery, weaves, pottery and items of rare craftsmanship and beauty.

King Anangpal of the Tomars built the citadel of Lalkot and ruled from the place where the Qutb Minar stands today. The ruins of Lalkot lie over an extensive area with the ramparts of the fort winding into the distance. The citadel was extended by Prithviraj Chauhan who also built several palaces and

Right & Facing page: The Qutb Minar marks the beginning of Muslim rule in India by the Turks in the late twelfth century. The tower stands 72.5 metres high amidst the ruins of Lalkot, the first historical city of Delhi. Built by Qutub-ud-din Aibak, it is an amalgam of the Hindu and Muslim styles of architecture which was to characterize the next 600 years of Delhi's history.

temples and called the area Qila Rai Pithora. Prithviraj Chauhan was a great conqueror and was looked upon as one of the greatest rulers of northern India. Because of his heroic exploits he even won the heart of an enemy's daughter Sanyogita who married him against her father's dictates.

The Rajputs under Prithviraj Chauhan, were defeated by Mohammad Ghori, the Turkish invader in A.D. 1192. For the first time in history a Muslim Kingdom was established in Delhi under his slaves. Qutub-ud-din Aibak declared himself a Sultan in A.D. 1206 and the kingdom came to be known as the Delhi Sultanate. The Slave Dynasty also gave India its first woman ruler—Razia Begum. Though her father Iltutmish found her to be wise and capable and as a ruler she was a great administrator, the Muslim nobility could not reconcile to being ruled by a woman. Moreover, the masses could not accept her public appearances without a veil and she was soon deposed.

For the next 600 years, Delhi was under Muslim rule and this brought about drastic changes in the original art, architecture, literature and lifestyle of the people of Delhi. There evolved a new ethos—a blend of the Hindu and the Muslim which can still be seen today.

The Qutb Minar, the tower of victory, and Delhi's best known landmark stands seventy-two metres above the ruins of the early kingdoms of Delhi. It is an amalgam of the Hindu and Muslim styles of architecture—the Hindu past evident in the carvings on the stones used for the buildings.

The surrounding areas of Mehrauli are dotted with some samples of early Muslim architecture as well as with some modern masterpieces of architecture. Just behind the Qutb is the Mahavir park with an exquisite statue of the Jain Saint. You can walk through the Qudsia park and the narrow lanes of a

As urban Delhi spread, it absorbed within its fold several villages which continue to retain their own distinct identity in the midst of the metropolitan hustle-bustle.

bustling bazaar of Mehrauli to feel the romance of a bygone era.

With the end of the Slave dynasty in A.D 1290, the focus shifted to a new city. Ala-ud-din Khilji, A.D. 1296-1316, was the most famous ruler of the Khilji dynasty and he left a definitive stamp on the history of Delhi. For the first time, Muslim rule spread beyond the boundaries of Delhi as he conquered most of Northern India as far as Gujarat, Ranthambhor, Chanderi, Malwa, Dhar and Ujjain. He even tried to conquer Mewar, the most powerful state of Rajputana. His need to invade Mewar was prompted by the fact that he was passionately in love with Padmini, the Queen of Rana Ratan Singh, renowned for her exceptional beauty. When the Rana died fighting, his beautiful queen immolated herself along with the other Rajput women of the court.

Ala-ud-din Khilji was also endowed with an aesthetic sense and a zeal to build. He built himself a new capital at Siri fortifying the area to form what is now called Siri Fort. Though little remains of his city today—the area is famous for the large, state-of-the-art auditorium, built in 1982 when the Asian Games were held in Delhi for the second time. The Siri Fort Auditorium is used for all major performances, and film festivals. The complex also has four restaurants serving Chinese, Indian and Continental cuisine.

To supply running water to the inhabitants of Siri, Ala-ud-din Khilji had built a reservoir— Hauz Khas. Adjoining the reservoir, Feroze Shah Tughlaq, the founder of the fifth city of Delhi built a university and a library. The village that grew around the ruins has been converted into a tourist complex. A tourist can wind his way through narrow mud-plastered lanes, avoiding the cows and buffaloes roaming free, and then enter through the door into the perfumed interior of the boutiques selling designer clothes, antiques,

A study in contrasts—the high-rise buildings and modern means of transport co-exist with rural traditions, making the city a unique blend of the old and the new.

21

Top: *A modern masterpiece of architecture—a gigantic statue of Mahavir, a Jain saint, located near the Qutb Minar complex.* *Above*: *The pillar that stands in the courtyard of the Qutb complex is made of a special metal, apparently impervious to rust, as it has remained unblemished over the centuries. Stand with your back against the pillar and extend your arms backwards and try to make your hands meet. If you can do that, any wish you make will come true.*
Facing page: *The President's Bodyguard, dressed in ceremonial uniforms and mounted on horses, at the gates of Rashtrapati Bhawan.* *Pages 24-25*: *A view of the city of Delhi from the minaret of Jama Masjid. The high-rise buildings of New Delhi can be seen in the background.*

jewellery, leather goods, and furniture. One can eat at any of the several restaurants and visit the ruins at dusk when the medieval structures are lit up and are used as a backdrop for folk dance performances.

The Khilji kingdom was overthrown in A.D. 1320 by the Tughlaqs and the activity shifted to the third medieval city of India—Tughlaqabad which was built in the short span of five years. One can explore the ramparts of the majestic fort which today serve as the shooting range for target practice by the army and the sportsmen. Muhammed bin Tughlaq described alternately as 'madman' and 'genius' by historians was one of the most extraordinary rulers of Delhi.. In 1326 he decided to move his capital to Daulatabad in South India, more centrally situated in his empire. But instead of shifting his government, he ordered all the inhabitants of Delhi to move to Daulatabad. And when his experiment failed, he marched them all back again, causing immense misery to his subjects. He then built himself a capital near Siri and called it Jahanpanah.

But it was Feroze Shah Tughlaq who left a mark on the architecture of present day Delhi. A scholar, architect and philanthropist, he built schools, mosques, palaces, bridges, monumental pillars and hospitals. And he built what has come to be known as Feroze Shah Kotla—the fifth city of Delhi, a thriving cultural and intellectual centre. The grounds around the fort are the scene of all cricket matches in Delhi. And every year in October, the Shri Ram Bharatiya Kala Kendra stages a ballet called the Ramlila or the story of Rama. Just a stone's throw away is the present day intellectual hub of the capital—Delhi's very own Fleet Street where every major newspaper in the country has an office.

Feroze Shah's city was plundered and ravaged by Timur Lane from Central Asia in 1398. It took the city many months to recover from the invasion. In fact the Lodhis even moved the capital to Agra, though not without contributing to the architectural magnificence of Delhi. Inside the sprawling lawns of the Lodhi Gardens in the heart of the present city of Delhi are several tombs of the Lodhi rulers.

The Lodhis were defeated by Babur, a descendant of Chengiz Khan and Timur at the historic battle of Panipat in 1526. His reign however was the beginning of a dynasty that was to rule India for the next 300 years, bringing about dramatic changes in art, culture as well as in the administration of the country. Of course, the establishment of their rule was not without its vicissitudes. Babur, the perfect soldier, was greatly devoted to his son Humayun. It is said that Humayun had fallen very ill and Babur prayed for him to get well, even circumambulating his bed seven times to take upon himself the illness. As Humayun got well, Babur began to fall ill and died a few days later.

Humayun, the second Mughal ruler planned to build a capital to rival Samarkand and name it Dinpanah, in the vicinity

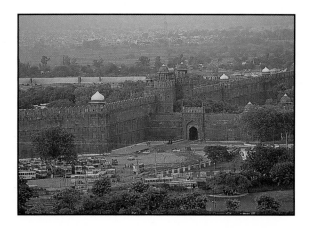

Top: India Gate—a memorial to an unknown soldier stands at one end of Rajpath. The extensive lawns around it are popular for evening promenades. *Middle*: The Jama Masjid, the largest mosque in India built by Emperor Shah Jahan, in the 1650s, across the road from his fort in Shahjahanabad, is an awesome monument. *Above*: A symbol of the splendour and magnificence of the Mughal empire—the Red Fort encloses within its walls marble palaces, a mosque, the Halls of Public and Private Audience and extensive gardens.

of the ancient city of the Pandavas—Indraprastha. His plans, however, were foiled by the wily Sher Shah Suri and he had to flee India. Though Sher Shah ruled only for a few years before Humayun returned to rule, he built the Purana Qila (on the site of Dinpanah), the ramparts of which spread over two kilometres. The massive sandstone gate is topped by cupolas and inside the fort is the two storeyed octagonal tower, the Sher Mandal. The Qila-e-Kuhna Masjid with the arched bays marks an evolution in the construction of a mosque—a transition from pre-Mughal styles to a distinctive new architectural style later adopted by the Mughals.

Inside the Purana Qila is the Museum of the Archaeological Survey of India which houses artefacts from ancient as well as medieval India. Today the Purana Qila stands surrounded by lovely parks, a lake where you can paddle-boat and acres of wooded area housing the Delhi Zoological gardens. Across the road is Pragati Maidan or the Trade Fair Ground. Built in 1972, its sprawling acres house several permanent exhibitions and are the venue for thematic exhibitions through the year. Within the complex is the Crafts Museum—a repository of traditional crafts and objects used in everyday life.

Humayun came back to rule from his dream city—by then Purana Qila, though he was not destined to live long. He enjoyed his throne for only six months when he slipped and fell down the library steps (Sher Mandal) and died. Down the road from the Purana Qila is the tomb of Humayun, the second Mughal King of Delhi—built by his Queen Haji Begum. The massive octagonal structure with geometrical marble patterns, high arches, *chhattris* and the marble dome with a spire have given it the name of Delhi's Taj. It was the forerunner of all the garden tombs of the Mughals with their Char Bagh pattern consisting of a grid of squares with channels and fountains.

On the outskirts of the historic Indraprastha, opposite Humayun's tomb is the *dargah* (shrine) of Hazrat Nizamuddin. This Sufi saint was made famous by his illustrious disciple, the poet Amir Khusrau. The Dargah and the Marble Mosque are surrounded by a *basti* (settlement) and hundreds of restaurants. While here you must eat at Karim's—for traditional Mughal fare. During the days of Urs, a festival dedicated to the memory of a saint, well known *qawwals* (*qawwali* is a form of semi-classical singing) sing in praise of the divine graces of the saint. Nizamuddin also has the Ghalib Academy—named after the famous poet of the nineteenth century—the venue of seminars and poetry readings.

After Humayun died, his son Akbar, the greatest of the Mughals shifted his capital to Agra. Imperial glory returned to Delhi in the reign of Akbar's grandson, Shah Jahan, who built the most magnificent Delhi of all—Shahjahanabad—the seventh city of Delhi. The city had fourteen gates, the majestic Lal Qila on the banks of the Yamuna, palaces, bazaars, gardens and the marble mosque, the largest in India, the Jama Masjid.

Shahjahanabad flourished until 1739 when Nadir Shah, the Persian invader plundered Delhi. Thousands of people were massacred in one day. He stayed in Delhi for two months and looted the bazaars, the markets, the treasury, and seized the Peacock Throne and the famous Kohinoor diamond.

Three and a half centuries ago the city of Shahjahanabad was a spacious one where princes and princesses rode in palanquins in gracious style. Today, the roads are full of cycles, bullocks, rickshaws, pedestrians, autorickshaws, four wheelers and even camels and elephants, and the shops stock large quantities of cloth, oil, grain, paper, trinkets, jewellery, sweetmeats—all ingredients for the magic and mystery of an oriental market.

Chandni Chowk today is for those who do not fear crowds, colour, smells and noise. The best way to explore the area is on foot—keeping clear of gutters, weaving in and out of narrow lanes. You can walk through Dariba Kalan—the street of silversmiths and goldsmiths, descended from those who served the Mughal courtiers; Kinari Bazaar off Dariba Kalan sells all the glitter required for a wedding; Paranthewali Gali sells the most appetizing eatables; and you can visit Ghantewala, the famous sweetshop established in 1790.

Jama Masjid was Shah Jahan's final achievement. It is an awesome monument and the area around it is vibrant and fascinating. As you approach the mosque, you encounter the many smells of the bazaars—fish, goats, foodstalls, perfume stalls, wedding saris, masks and *Masq ka pani*—water distributed from goatskin bags. The pavement hawkers, small shopkeepers, zari workers, booksellers, ivory carvers and travelling valets are all inhabitants of the walled city who belong to another era.

The Red Fort which took nine years to build and cost one crore rupees is open to the public everyday. Apart from the marble palaces and the halls of Public and Private Audience, the riverside fort houses a museum which has all the Mughal artefacts. Today, in the evenings, a sound and light show brings to life the splendour and magnificence of the Mughal empire. You can top off the day by eating at Karim's Nemat Kada, who claim to have been the chefs of the Mughal emperors.

Delhi soon spread beyond the walls of Shahjahanabad towards the ridge in the north where the British camped before taking over the city in 1857. And into Darya Ganj towards Feroze Shah's deserted city. Today the whole area thrives with commercial activity. The pavements of Darya Ganj host a book bazaar every Sunday. And behind the Red Fort along the Ring Road facing the Yamuna is the Sunday Bazaar or the Chor Bazaar which is a flea market. Close to it are the memorials to modern Indian leaders—Mahatma Gandhi, Jawaharlal Nehru, Indira Gandhi and Rajiv Gandhi—havens of peace and greenery in the midst of the

Top: The crumbling ramparts of the Purana Qila—the Old Fort built by Sher Shah Suri on the site of the Pandava's capital, Indraprastha. The surrounding areas house the zoological gardens and a lake where you can go boating. **Middle**: The tomb of Humayun, the second Mughal emperor, is an architectural wonder, and is also known as Delhi's Taj. Architecturally, it was the forerunner of all garden tombs of the Mughal dynasty. **Above**: A relic of the twilight years of the Mughal rule—the marble and sandstone Safdarjung tomb was the last of the mausoleums of the Mughal dynasty.

hustle and bustle of the city.

In 1857, following the first war of Indian Independence when the Indian rulers united to fight the British, the last Mughal King Bahadurshah Zafar was deposed and deported to Burma. The British ruled from the Red Fort until the new capital was built.

Edwin Lutyens, a renowned architect of stately homes in England was assigned the distinctive task of designing and building the new capital—Delhi's eighth and present city. He built a fortress like palace atop Raisina Hill with a panoramic view of the new city—The Viceroy's House, the splendid Rashtrapati Bhawan, surrounded by office blocks and official residences.

Around the Rashtrapati Bhawan, the Secretariat Buildings, the Parliament House, India Gate and Connaught Place there has grown a large city, the largest in India which is the political, bureaucratic, cultural and business capital of the country.

The centre of all activity in New Delhi is Connaught Place which is a mix of a shops, office blocks, restaurants and hotels. Over the years the shops have changed hands, new restaurants have appeared, interiors have been modernized and the tall pillared corridors have been dwarfed by the high-rise buildings that now form the commercial complex in Connaught Place.

While the shops in the inner circle are upmarket, the bazaars on Janpath and the underground market—Palika Bazaar offer bargain shopping. Janpath, earlier known as Queensway has small shops selling the latest European and American fashions, silk, brassware, leatherware, books and Tibetan trinkets.

Down Parliament Street, one of the roads off Connaught Place you come across a collection of strange looking large stone structures called Jantar

*Above: Connaught Place, the centre of all activity in New Delhi—a great shopping and office complex, built by Lutyens. **Facing page**: Three and a half centuries ago Shajahanabad was a spacious promenade for royalty who rode in palanquins in gracious style. Today the roads are full of all kinds of traffic and Chandni Chowk is a crowded business and commercial centre.*

Mantar. Built by Sawai Jai Singh II, a ruler of Jaipur and a scholar of astronomy, these instruments were used to study the movements of the planets.

A kilometre away from Connaught Place is Mandi House, the cultural heartland of Delhi, teeming with aspiring actors, musicians, dancers, artists, sculptors and puppeteers. You can have a snack at the famous Tea Terrace of Triveni—the home of three streams of art—music, dance and painting. You must also sample the snack foods available at Bengali Market.

India Gate is the Arc de Triomphe of Delhi and Rajpath its Champs-Elysées leading upto the Rashtrapati Bhawan. Up Rajpath is what is called the Boat Club. Located in the heart of Lutyens' Delhi, the several hundred acres of lawn are used for all political rallies in the capital. Around India Gate are two of Delhi's most prestigious museums. The National Museum has over 150,000 works of art, several galleries exhibiting pre-historical, and archaeological sculptures, paintings, coins, musical instruments, arms, armour, textiles and the latest addition—an exclusive gallery of jewellery. In addition to these permanent exhibitions are the short term thematic exhibitions and daily film shows and talks on subjects of historical and artistic interest. The National Gallery of Modern Art is next to the India Gate lawns situated in Jaipur House. The gallery has an extensive collection of contemporary paintings, sculptures and graphic art.

Above: The lotus shaped marble Baha'i temple illuminated at night.
Facing page: *The Moti Masjid or the Pearl Mosque—a pure marble structure within the Red Fort at Delhi.*

Adding to the wealth of the ancient and medieval cities of Delhi are present day architectural wonders like the Baha'i temple. Set amidst sprawling landscaped gardens, the lotus shaped marble structure has a large hall for meditation offering peace and quiet—very close to the hectic activity at the near by commercial complex of Nehru Place.

Lutyens' architectural extravaganza

New Delhi was an architectural extravaganza, an attempt by the British to legitimize their rule of the Indian subcontinent. In 1911 it was decided to build a new capital, and Sir Edwin Lutyens and Sir Herbert Baker were appointed to create a city that would be a spectacular symbol of the British Empire.

The centrepiece of this magnificent city was the Viceroy's House, now known as the Rashtrapati Bhawan, a 300 room presidential palace—the largest in the world, spread over five acres. The inside of the
palace is as exquisite as the outside. Chandeliers from Belgium, marble from Italy, teakwood from Burma have been used to create this masterpiece of architecture. The palace is open to visitors on Mondays, Wednesdays and Fridays between 8 to 10 a.m. and 4 to 6.30 p.m. Entry is only by prior approval of the Invitation Section of Rashtrapati Bhawan. Foreign tourists have to approach through a tourist agency and should be sponsored by their Embassy. Photography is not permitted.

The Rashtrapati Bhawan flanked by the Secretariat buildings illuminated for special occasions.

The large dome of Rashtrapati Bhawan looms over the Secretariat buildings of North and South Blocks where all the major policy decisions are made and where the Prime Minister has his office. The Parliament House—the circular building a little way from the Rashtrapati Bhawan was built in 1921 as an afterthought when Lutyens was told that the government had conceded a legislature for India.

From the Rashtrapati Bhawan, through the two Secretariat Buildings, you can see Vijay Chowk and from there the Rajpath leads to India Gate—a grand memorial to the unknown soldier.

Lutyens also built Connaught Place—the grand old lady with the once staid corridors now bursting at the seams. Lutyens' architectural strategy however prevents the density of crowds from becoming overbearing.

New Delhi's office and residence buildings are surrounded by acres and acres of sprawling lawns, avenues shaded by large trees, giving it the title of the greenest capital in the world.

Agra
The mainstage of the Mughals

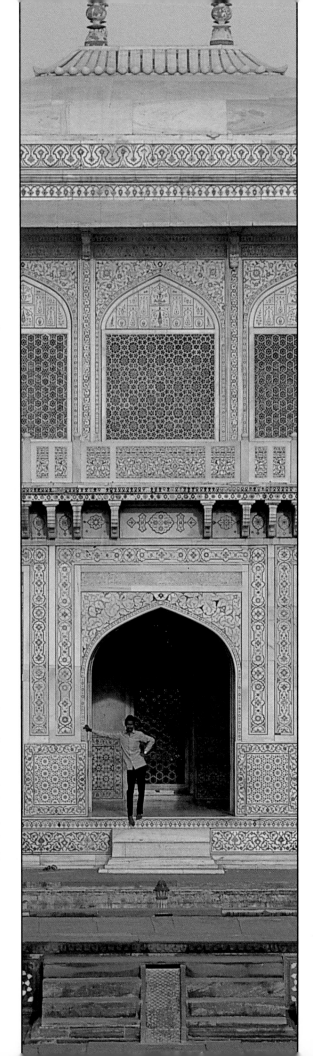

The name of Agra, the legendary city of the Taj, has its roots in ancient Hindu myths where it was known as Agraban—Sanskrit for paradise. Agra was a rich pastoral village and in the fourteenth century, the Lodhis moved their capital here from Delhi to better control their kingdom. The Lodhis built their fort where now Sikandra—the mausoleum of Akbar, the greatest Mughal stands.

Babur, a soldier, statesman, adventurer and diarist from Samarkand invaded India and defeated the Lodhis at the historic battle of Panipat in 1526, and laid the foundations of the greatest dynasty to have ruled India. The Mughals ruled from Delhi and Agra for the next 300 years leaving behind a rich legacy of art, architecture, music as well as a strong administrative system that united India for the first time in history.

Agra remained their mainstage for over a century and they made it into a true paradise (as the ancient name of the city suggests) embellishing it with palaces, forts, gardens and that truly magnificent monument to love—the Taj Mahal. The dazzling splendour of the court included glittering courtiers, bedecked in jewel-encrusted dresses, queens who discovered how to capture and distil the scent of rose petals, and a ceremony where twice a year the emperor was weighed in gold and silver which was then distributed to the people.

When Babur first came to India he found the heat of the plains unbearable and the living conditions primitive. He missed the mountainous terrain of his homeland, the thoroughbred horses, the food, the bazaars and the colleges. To make his new kingdom less oppressive, he laid out a beautiful garden in true Persian style with canals, fountains and pathways. He also built a subterranean palace to live in. The garden today is called Ram Bagh, but there is no trace of his palace under the ground.

It was Akbar, Babur's grandson, the grandest Mughal of all who established Mughal supremacy in India. Through military conquests he united most of India under his sovereignty, and extended his empire from Gujarat to Bengal and from Kashmir to Ahmednagar in the Deccan. By establishing strategic

Right: Itmad-ud-daulah—the tomb built by Nur Jahan for her father, Mirza Ghiyas has the first examples of inlay work on a Mughal structure. The work was later perfected by Shah Jahan at the Taj Mahal.
Facing page: The palaces and monuments built by Shah Jahan were made of marble with intricate motifs in inlay work. *Overleaf*: The pristine purity of the marble at the Taj makes it the most exquisite monument in the world. In the background is the mosque built on one side of the Taj.

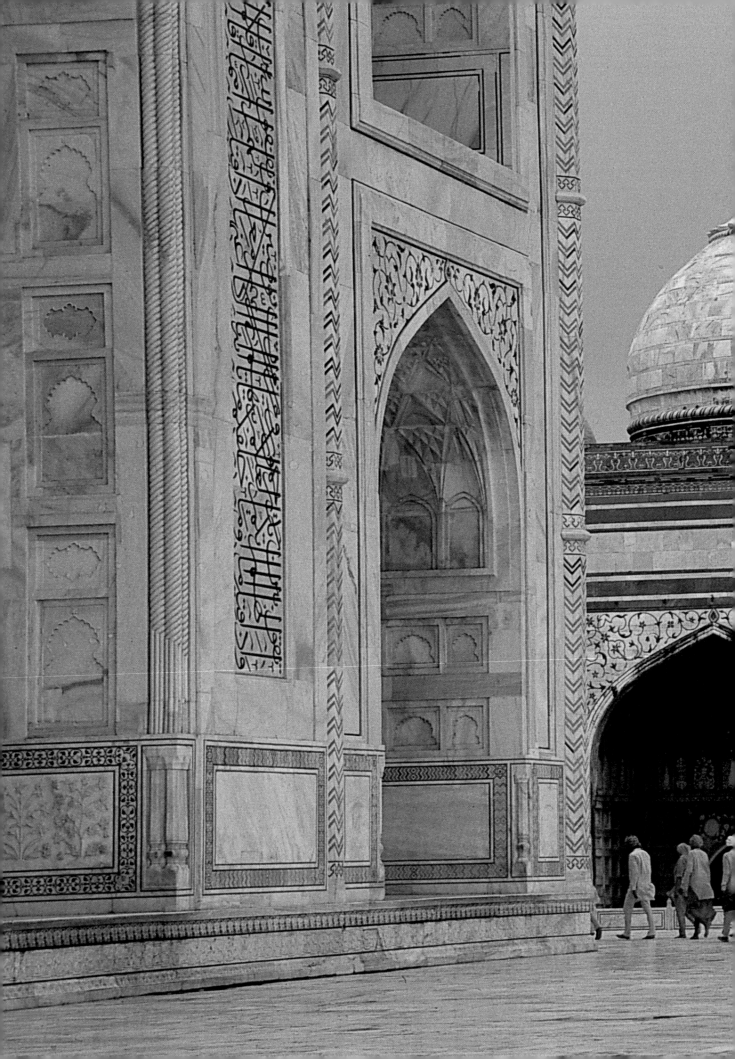

alliances with the existing rulers, he was able to establish a framework of administration which brought peace and order to his empire. Like a true statesman Akbar gave up the policy of discrimination and adopted a policy of conciliation towards the Hindus. He married the daughter of Raja Bihari Mal of Amber and in 1570 married two Rajput princesses of Bikaner and Jaisalmer. Several Rajputs and Hindus were given positions of responsibility. Raja Bhagawan Das and Raja Man Singh were his military commanders. Raja Todar Mal was his finance minister and Birbal his most trusted advisor.

He made Agra the seat of imperial power and ruled from within the massive sandstone walls of the Red Fort which he built. The main gate of the fort has a drawbridge that was raised at night. It was only the privileged few who were allowed to enter beyond the gate. The forbidding walls of the fort enclose The Hall of Public Audience (which later housed Shah Jahan's peacock throne), the exquisite palaces, the treasury, the gardens and the apartments of the royal harem. New buildings were added by the successive rulers. It is easy to see the three distinct architectural styles of Akbar, Jahangir and Shah Jahan, the Emperors who made the greatest contribution to the buildings. Within the fort, Akbar's style was stark and definitive with a liberal sprinkling of Hindu motifs reflecting his strong personality and secular inclination. Jahangir and Shah Jahan favoured a more romantic and sensuous style, decorating the palaces with marble and inlaying them with precious and semi precious stones in delicate floral designs—the *pietra dura*. The most delicate work is in the Musamman Burj, a mini palace built by Shah Jahan intended for Mumtaz Mahal. It was here that he was later imprisoned by his son Aurangzeb. And from here that he

***Above**: The Taj Mahal, as seen from the Agra Fort. In his last years, Emperor Shah Jahan was held prisoner within his palace by his son Aurangzeb. His only solace was that he could see the Taj from his window.*

gazed forlornly at the distant Taj until his death.

The Mughal Court under Akbar was famous for its markets which boasted carpets, silks, gems and gold cloth. Agra became an important centre for artisans; jewellers and traders from all over the country who were attracted to it by its riches. It was also a cultural and intellectual centre with poets, artists and musicians receiving lavish patronage. Ambassadors from Europe came to verify stories of the glorious kingdom. Writers wrote rich accounts of the splendour of the Mughal court and traders came to seek its wealth. Ralph Fitch, arriving in 1584, was one of the first English merchants to come in search of trade. Travellers wrote brilliantly descriptive diaries. Accounts included those by Peter Mundy, who watched the Taj Mahal being built; and Niccolao Manucci, an Italian quack-doctor, who livened his observations with gossip. It was truly a fairy tale court—rich and extravagant.

The British envoy Sir Thomas Roe, sent by James I sought trading rights from Surat and received a royal firman to this effect in 1615—during the reign of Jahangir—who preferred the life of luxury and opium drinking to administration. Sir Thomas Roe in his journal describes the lavish parties and the pomp and splendour for which Jahangir's court was famous. The kingdom was ruled by his beautiful queen Nur Jahan—'the Light of the World'. She was the daughter of an ambitious Persian adventurer who became the Chief Minister to Emperor Jahangir. This family gave the Mughals two of their most renowned queens—Nur Jahan and her brother's daughter Arjumand—Mumtaz Mahal. Nur Jahan ruled the kingdom with the proverbial iron hand with the help of her father who came to be known as Itmad-ud-daulah—'the Pillar of the State'.

Above: The open balcony outside the Diwan-e-khas at Agra Fort which has Jahangir's throne, carved out of a single block of black marble.
Overleaf: A view of the palaces, halls, gardens and mosques inside the massive sandstone Agra Fort— the imperial seat of power of the Mughals for nearly 150 years.

When Itmad-ud-daulah died, Nur Jahan built for him the most exquisite tomb across the Yamuna from the Taj near Ram Bagh, Babur's garden and palace. The four gateways in red sandstone give way to a Persian garden in true Char Bagh style. And in the centre is a small marble structure with octagonal towers that appears to be a delicate casket. It is inlaid with coloured stones, on the outside and decorated with rich murals inside. The exquisite surface decoration in *pietra dura* is the first of its kind on such a scale. This style was later borrowed and perfected by Shah Jahan when he built the Taj Mahal for his beloved queen.

Shah Jahan who came to the throne in 1628 was the most lavish builder of all. Inheriting an overflowing treasury and struck by tragedy early during his reign when Mumtaz Mahal died giving birth to their fourteenth child—the king threw himself into frenzied building activity. He created the Peacock throne, made of solid silver and encrusted with emeralds and diamonds. In 1638, Shah Jahan moved to Delhi to create the magnificent Shahjahanabad, but before he left Agra he created some of Mughal India's most marvellous masterpieces.

Within the Agra Fort, he built the Moti Masjid or the Pearl Mosque. And two kilometres downstream he created the most beautiful and evocative building in the world, the Taj Mahal, in memory of his beloved queen Mumtaz Mahal. Shah Jahan had fallen in love with the princess Arjumand Banu at first sight when he met her in a royal bazaar. He asked his father's permission to marry her—which was readily given. At the wedding she was given the title of Mumtaz Mahal or 'Light of the palace'. She was Shah Jahan's constant companion even accompanying him on his military campaigns for the seventeen years of their marriage. When she died he was grief stricken and according to historians aged overnight.

Thousands of artisans were employed and no cost spared to create this glorious monument which strongly reflects the imagery of paradise. The large marble dome represents the vault of heaven, the square platform upon which it rests the material universe and the octagonal towers the transitional phase. The tomb has been lavishly ornamented with calligraphy which includes verses from the Quran. The pristine purity of the white marble glimmers and is clearly reflected in the canals reminiscent of paradise. No photograph can capture the spirit or the ethereal beauty of this structure nor can any description do it justice. Every person has to experience the Taj for himself.

Inside the Taj Mahal the cenotaphs of Shah Jahan and Mumtaz Mahal rest enclosed by an exquisitely carved octagonal latticed screen of marble. The cenotaphs are inlaid with floral motifs in precious stones. In one case, thirty five different stones have been used on a single bloom. The priceless treasures of the Taj—Turkish and Persian carpets, gold cloth, lamp with gold chains and the priceless pearl

Top: A view of the Sikandra gateway with the minarets at the four corners of the monument. ***Middle****: Set in the midst of a small garden is the jewel-box like tomb of Itmad-ud-daulah, the Prime Minister and father-in-law of Emperor Jahangir.* ***Above****: Similar in style to the Panch Mahal at Fatehpur Sikri, Akbar's tomb at Sikandra has no parallel. The five-storey structure is like a pyramid without a top.* ***Facing page****: The exquisite workmanship on the interior walls of Akbar's tomb at Sikandra, ten kilometres from Agra.* ***Following pages 44-45****: Seen through arches, the Taj Mahal appears to be floating on a sea of clouds.* ***Pages 46-47****: The Taj stands in its pristine glory on the banks of the Yamuna awaiting the rise of another day.*

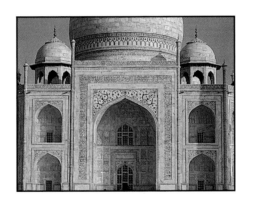

THE TAJ MAHAL WAS BUILT BETWEEN 1631 AND 1653 BY EMPEROR SHAH JAHAN (1627-1658) AS THE TOMB FOR HIS WIFE ARJUMAND, BETTER KNOWN AS MUMTAZ MAHAL, "ORNAMENT OF THE PALACE", BORN IN 1592, THE DAUGHTER OF ASAF KHAN, SHE MARRIED SHAH JAHAN IN 1612 AND DIED IN 1631 AFTER THE BIRTH OF HER FOURTEENTH CHILD. AFTER HIS DEATH THE EMPEROR WAS BURIED BY HER SIDE.

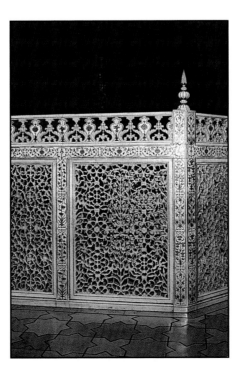

***Facing page (top to bottom)**:*
In the early morning light, the Taj looks illusory and other worldly—a mirage.
An aerial view of the Taj—a jewel on the banks of the Yamuna.
The large marble dome connects heaven and earth.
Seen through the mist, the Taj aquires a soft look.
The Taj is at its best in the monsoons when the sky darkens with the rainclouds and the monument is washed clean by the heavy rains.
Thousands of artisans were employed to create this glorious monument. Its perfect symmetry and eye for detail awes the visitors.
The pure marble acquires a soft glimmer in the late evening light.
The subtle changes in the light through the day present the Taj in different moods.
***This page (top to bottom)**: Verses from the Quran have been inlaid into the marble gateways of the Taj. The architects have repeatedly used the arch set within a rectangle to give the monument its symmetry. Reaching for the heavens, the entrance to the Taj Mahal. Mumtaz Mahal rests in splendour, her cenotaph fabulously inlaid with precious and semi-precious stones. The exquisitely carved octagonal latticed screen in marble encloses the cenotaphs of Mumtaz Mahal and Shah Jahan.*

49

canopy were all stolen in the last years of Mughal rule. It is said that Shah Jahan wanted to build another tomb across the Yamuna in black marble and join the two with a silver bridge. But there is no evidence to support this version.

If the Taj Mahal is ethereal and other worldly, Akbar's tomb ten kilometres away at Sikandra is a symbol of the steadfastness and quiet dignity that marked the rule of this great Mughal. Akbar had began to build his mausoleum during his lifetime but it was completed in 1613, eight years after his death, by his son Jahangir. The base of the structure is in earthy sandstone typifying Akbar's style and the embellishments added on by Jahangir are in pure marble.

But the greatest architectural achievement of Akbar was his dream city atop the ridge at Sikri, the emperor's, tribute to the sufi saint, Sheikh Salim Chisti. Emperor Akbar and his queen, Jodhabai made a pilgrimage to Sikri to seek the blessings of the same when the Emperor was childless. With the blessing of Salim Chisti, three sons were born to Akbar. He named his first born Salim after the saint. In 1571, Akbar built his magnificent capital and embellished it with palaces. The mosque was the first structure to be built.

Aerial view of Fatehpur Sikri, the city built by Emperor Akbar in 1571, as a tribute to the Sufi Saint—Salim Chisti whose blessings enabled Akbar to get a son and heir to the throne.

50

In the courtyard is the tomb of Salim Chisti, an exquisite structure in marble with gorgeous ornamentation.

Fatehpur Sikri was Akbar's imperial capital for fifteen years though Agra remained the military stronghold. Sikri was his personal dream, his artistic and intellectual centre.

After Akbar conquered Gujarat, he built the Buland Darwaza—a victory gate rising 176 feet from the ground. In 1585, Fatehpur Sikri was deserted and the splendid edifice rests in quiet peace—a perfect ghost city declared a World Heritage Monument.

The city of Agra 200 kilometres south of Delhi is a city of beautiful buildings, surrounded by narrow serpentine lanes. It has crowded bazaars and the quiet cantonment built by the British when they made it the capital of the North—West Province in 1830.

Today Agra is a bustling, noisy town catering mainly to the thousands of tourists that descend upon it attracted by the surreal beauty of the Taj Mahal. At the same time it is famous for its foundries, shoe making, leather craft and the exquisite inlay work on marble—replicating the most magnificent monument in the world.

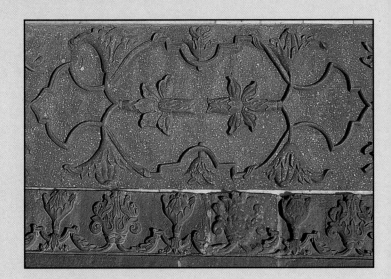

Artistry in stone

The Mughals have left behind some magnificent monuments which were not only majestic and grandiose in proportion, but have intricate carvings and exquisite decorations. This eye for detail and the exceptional craftsmanship resulted in perfect artistry.

The early Mughal monuments are embellished with mosaic work which was prevalent in India before their arrival. With the development of Mughal architecture, the decorative work was refined and perfected. Fatehpur Sikri has exquisite carvings in stone, and Sikandra has marble inlay work which was to reach its zenith in the two most magnificent monuments in Agra—The Itmad-ud-daulah and the Taj Mahal.

Across the river from The Taj is the Chini Ka Rauza, the tomb of the Finance Minister of Shah Jahan, Shukurullah Shirazi, which has been decorated with famous porcelain tiles in fantastic designs.

The art of marble inlay also known as pietra dura originated in Florence in the sixteenth century. During Akbar's reign the Mughals were exposed to European art and ideas. And this exquisite art form used on small plates, and boxes made its way to India. The Mughals with their penchant for extravagance adopted the style to create magnificent monuments.

It was Nur Jahan, Jahangir's powerful wife who in her quest to create beauty invited the Italian artists to embellish the tomb of her father, Itmad-ud-daulah. The tomb has the most prolific decoration of pietra dura, the first of this kind on such a scale. The jewel-box like mausoleum is covered with pieces of precious and semi-precious stones in geometrical and floral patterns.

This art was perfected by Shah Jahan on the Taj Mahal.

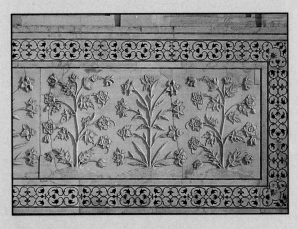

*Top left: Chini ka Rauza—an example of the porcelain glazed tile decoration. **Middle**: The decorations on the Taj represent the many flowers that were planted in the gardens. **Bottom**: Exquisite craftsmanship on marble at the Taj. **Above**: Agra Fort—carving on sandstone.*

The walls, the cenotaphs, the screen and the exteriors are covered with inlay work in onyx, cornelian, lapis lazuli, topaz and jasper in refined floral and Persian motifs. In one place a single bloom has been inlaid with thirty five different stones.

The patronage of the inlay industry by the Mughals continued until the eighteenth century when along with the decline of the dynasty, the art form began to die out. No one has the kind of money and leisurely lifestyle to afford such luxury, though there have been attempts to revive the art and create a demand.

The craftsmen, only a handful survive now, all live in Agra, the only place the art is practiced now. For them it is a family tradition handed down from father to son, and it takes years of practice to perfect the skill requiring sharp eyes and dexterous hands. First the design is cut on a brass plate and then traced on marble. The marble is then carved and the slivers of precious stone which have been shaped and polished inlaid into marble with adhesive. After it dries, it is polished until it shines. A bow saw strung with copper wire is used to slice and cut stones.

The scale on which this art is practised now has been miniaturized. From the monumental works decorated by their ancestors, the craftsmen today make small boxes, pill boxes, plates, table tops and wall hangings of marble inlaid with stones. The art however continues to be as intricate and pleasing to the eye as it was in the sixteenth century.

The monuments built by the Mughals are awesome in size, a constant reminder of the grand dynasty and the extent of their glory. And the decoration of the monuments leave us speechless, giving us an insight into their creativity and aesthetic sense.

Above: Geometric patterns in marble inlay at the Itmad-ud-daulah.
Top right: Carving on a pillar at Fatehpur Sikri.
Middle: The introduction of the Persian style in inlay at the Itmad-ud-daulah. *Bottom*: Marble inlaid with precious stones at the Taj Mahal.

Jaipur
The royal city

The Kachwaha rulers of Amber claim descent from the Sun God through Kusa, who was the twin son of the god Rama. Warriors by caste, they came to settle in Rajputana in the twelfth century and soon established a powerful kingdom in the Aravalli Hills. Through exceptional military prowess and ingenious diplomatic alliances, they soon became the most powerful clan amongst the Rajputs and amassed enough wealth to create one of the richest treasuries in India.

Through the generations, the Kachwaha rulers served the Mughals, and commanded their armies to conquer far off provinces in India. Raja Bihari Mal was the first Rajput to forge an alliance with the Mughals by paying homage to Emperor Humayun and giving his daughter Jodhabai in marriage to Akbar—their son was Emperor Jahangir. Bihari Mal's adopted grandson Raja Man Singh served the Mughal army to become the Commander in Chief of Akbar's armies. His successors Raja Jai Singh I and Raja Jai Singh II served Jahangir, Shah Jahan and finally Aurangzeb. Jai Singh II was only eleven years old when he succeeded to the throne of Amber. When he met Aurangzeb the latter grasped his arms and said, 'Tell me what you deserve of me.' The child replied, 'When a bridegroom takes a bride's hand he is bound by duty to protect her all her life. Now that the Emperor has taken my hand, I have nothing to fear.' Impressed by the child's reply and well aware of the Rajput military acumen and the fierce loyalty of the Kachwahas, Aurangzeb bestowed upon them the title of 'Sawai' or 'One and a quarter' and gave them the right to fly an extra flag atop their fort making them truly superior to the other Rajput Kingdoms.

The martial nature of the Rajputs and the continuous warfare they engaged in necessitated the fortifying of their palaces and cities. The Kachwahas built for themselves the spectacular fort of Jaigarh on a high ridge and the medieval fort of Nahargarh, both easily accessible from the present city of Jaipur—and a convenient retreat in the case of an attack.

*Facing page: The City Palace in Jaipur, exquisitely decorated, retains its old charm as the erstwhile royal family still lives here. In the picture is one of the retainers of the palace standing beside a painting of one of the rulers. **Right**: An intricately ornamental facade, with 953 windows, the Hawa Mahal stands a little away from the City Palace but is an inherent part of it. **Overleaf**: Because of the constant warfare the Rajputs indulged in, they had to heavily fortify their living quarters. The Amber fort is built within a protective circle of the Aravalli hills.*

The Amber fort, the most exquisite fort of all, was built by Raja Man Singh, a total contrast to the earlier forts of Jaigarh and Nahargarh. While those were purely military strongholds, Amber was embellished with the most luxurious palaces and residences. The fort rambles over the rugged Aravallis which are reflected in the Maota Lake below. The fort is located very strategically, surrounded by a circle of hills forming a protective cover—no enemy could approach the fort without being seen. Along the hills are crenellated walls and look out posts which lead to the magnificent fort. The extremely powerful and commanding exterior gives way to the luxury and extravagance associated with the royal traditions of splendour.

At the entrance is the grand gateway, the Ganesh Pol, exquisitely carved and painted with frescoes—in a distinctly Mughal style of decoration. The gateway leads to the Hall of Public Audience with its cooling pools and cascades and a Hall of Mirrors which was the envy of the Mughals.

Vast courtyards give the feeling of space and separate the public and private areas. The women's quarters are even further inside through a maze of corridors away from the public gaze and difficult to access by the enemy if he were to enter the fort.

The interiors have been decorated to cool the palaces in the midst of the desert climate and to add colour and richness to the bleak surroundings. The walls are covered with panels of frescoes depicting peacocks, women, and flowers. The halls are decorated with mirrors. The lattice window screens let in the breeze but kept out the scorching sun; and passing over pools

Above: The City Palace, Jaipur with the seven-storeyed Chandra Mahal in the background.
Facing page: The Hawa Mahal— the delicate work on the structure gives it a romantic and fragile appearance.

Above: Colour is the essence of life in Jaipur—women dress in bright yellows, reds, pinks, blues and greens—the gaudier the better. **Top right**: A regally turbaned old man—turbans in vibrant colours and patterns are an essential part of a man's dress. **Middle**: A turbaned old man sells local savouries at the Jaleb Chowk at Amber. **Bottom**: A vegetable market at Jaipur.

Above: Craftsman at work. **Top**: All Rajasthani women keep their heads and in some cases, their faces covered with bright veils. **Middle**: The whole city was given a pink coat to welcome the Prince of Wales. The colour has stayed giving the city the nomenclature of the Pink City. **Bottom**: A bazaar near Hawa Mahal, filled with an array of colourful clothes adding an extra splash of colour to the Pink City.

61

and cascades, the air cooled the interiors.

After he had proved his military prowess and had been generously rewarded by Emperor Aurangzeb, Jai Singh II left the Mughal Court. Sawai Jai Singh achieved a diplomatic coup when he concluded an alliance with the ruler of Udaipur—his staunchest rival. Jai Singh married the Maharaja's daughter in return for unqualified support. The new queen was given special privileges and a guarantee that her son would be heir to the throne. In fact he built for her a special palace, the Sisodia Rani palace.

After the death of Aurangzeb, for the lack of a strong ruler, the Mughal nobility indulged in petty rivalries and court intrigues. Jai Singh II, the most illustrious Rajput ruler—soldier, statesman, scholar, builder, astronomer and master diplomat—decided to concentrate on his two passions in life—art and science. His diplomatic alliances gave him the confidence to leave his fortified capital at Amber and move to the plains where he founded the city of Jaipur in 1727. Built by Vidyadhar Bhattacharya, a renowned architect, Jaipur's architecture has aristocratic elegance and sophisticated town planning based on ancient Indian tenets laid down in the shastras.

Set within crenellated walls and huge gateways guarding the entrance, Jaipur is a colourful and vibrant city where the past overwhelms the present; a city of busting bazaars, living traditions and the pomp and splendour of royalty. When the city was built, merchants and craftsmen were invited to practice their trade, laying the foundations of the city as the gem and jewellery centre where precious stones are cut and set in exquisite designs; where bangle sellers make colourful bangles to fit your hands and suit your taste; where silversmiths craft the most intricate designs; where potters

Above: *The pure silver urn weighing 240 kilos is one of the pair carried by Sawai Madho Singh to England for the coronation of Edward VIII. He used them to store water so he would not have to drink water abroad. These urns are on display at the City Palace, Jaipur.*
Facing page: *The City Palace has several ornate gates; a royal retainer stands outside an elaborately decorated entrance.*

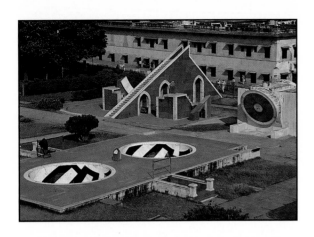

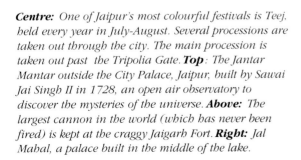

*Centre: One of Jaipur's most colourful festivals is Teej, held every year in July-August. Several processions are taken out through the city. The main procession is taken out past the Tripolia Gate. **Top**: The Jantar Mantar outside the City Palace, Jaipur, built by Sawai Jai Singh II in 1728, an open air observatory to discover the mysteries of the universe. **Above**: The largest cannon in the world (which has never been fired) is kept at the craggy Jaigarh Fort. **Right**: Jal Mahal, a palace built in the middle of the lake.*

Top: *Sisodia Rani Palace—outside Jaipur built for the Maharani from Udaipur.* **Above:** *The entrance gate to Jaipur city which until a few years ago was shut at 11 p.m., leaving visitors to the city arriving at night stranded outside city limits.* **Left:** *The City Palace has several intricately decorated balconies and corridors.*

*Top: The courtyard inside Amber Fort from where passages lead to the luxurious interiors. **Middle**: The Sheesh Mahal at Amber Fort is embedded with thousands of mirrors. The Rajputs used a lot of mirrors in their architecture, perhaps because they reflect like water—a scarce commodity in the desert. **Above**: A Rajasthani musician entertains the tourists—the music and ballads of the desert have a haunting, lilting quality and recount legends of the brave heroes of the land.*

fashion items of use and decoration painted in a special hue—the blue pottery of Jaipur. The political turbulence in northern India in the nineteenth century and the comparative peace of Jaipur attracted businessmen, moneylenders, jewellers giving a further impetus to Jaipur as a commercial centre. Every kind of craftsman was allotted an area—the silversmiths, the potters etc. They lived in the dwellings above the bazaars and entered their houses through bylanes. Today Jaipur is a treasure house of living arts and crafts.

The nerve centre of Jaipur is the City Palace—the largest structure in the city built by Sawai Jai Singh II. This is the royal residence to which every ruler has added some new buildings. The pristine white Mubarak Mahal was built in 1900 by Maharaja Madho Singh II as a guest house. Now it forms part of the City Palace Museum and is called the Tosha Khana (Royal Wardrobe). The rooms contain such extravagant outfits as the special black and gold Diwali festival dress, whose *odhni* (shawl) alone has eighteen pounds of gold woven into it. The wardrobe also contains Jaipur pottery, Mughal glass and musical instruments. However, the centre piece is the *atamsukh* of Madho Singh I. This raspberry-pink outfit of Banarsi silk, covered with gold *butti* (dots) clothed a man seven feet tall and over five hundred pounds. The inner rooms lead to the Chandra Mahal, the seven storey royal residence of the Maharajas even today. The Outer Palace is today a museum with an exquisite collection of carpets, paintings and old manuscripts and an array of medieval armoury. In the armoury, every kind of bejewelled dagger, sword, shield and gun is found. Jai Singh I of Amber's turban-shaped helmet and shield are specially opulent. There is also a steel mace in the shape of a lotus bud. Lodged in the victim's stomach, it would spring open into a fan of sharp spikes.

The Diwan-e-khas represents the synthesis of Mughal and Rajput architecture. On display are a pair of large urns made of 240 kilograms of silver specially created for Sawai Madho Singh when he was travelling to England for the Coronation of Edward VII. He used them to store water so that he would not be polluted by foreign water. The Diwan-i-Am now forms the focus of the Sawai Man Singh II Museum. Carpets from Lahore, Herat and Agra are displayed on the walls and royal palanquins, chandeliers, miniature paintings and manuscripts fill the room.

And away from the Palace but an inherent part of it is the Hawa Mahal—the best known example of fanciful architecture. Added to the main Palace structure in 1799 by Sawai Pratap Singh, the Hawa Mahal with its screened balconies, 953 niches and windows is whimsical in design. The five storey concrete curtain served to shield the royal women while they watched processions or festivities in the streets below. The delicate work on the structure gives it a romantic and fragile appearance—an ideal setting for the fairy tale story of Jaipur City.

Outside the main gateway is Jai Singh's Jantar Mantar, an open air observatory conceived by the astronomer king to discover the mysteries of the universe. It consists of several well proportioned instruments in stone which replaced the earlier metal instruments now displayed at the City Palace museum.

Jaipur's old city personifies its charm, vibrancy and life. The best way to explore the city is on foot through the Badi and Choti Chaupads designed by Sawai Jai Singh—with shops on all sides. The quadrangles in the centre form the plazas, which also served as the meeting ground as people took a stroll in the evenings. Today the Chaupads are very noisy, filled with all manner of traffic. Camels are predominant along with rickshaws, tempos, taxis, cars, buses, lorries. Many of the city's interesting shops are here. Trinkets, junk jewellery, fabric in the tie and dye and laharia styles, and bangles, spices and puppets are found here. The Choti Chaupad is the wholesale market for the agricultural products from the surrounding villages. In all this bustle, colour is the keynote. The women are dressed in bright yellow, pink, red, or blue and the men wear colourful turbans—the gaudier the better. Jaipur loves colour!

Jaipur, in fact, came to be known as the Pink City when Sawai Ram Singh spruced it up to welcome the Prince of Wales in 1876. He painted all the buildings pink, giving the royal city a romantic, delicate and fragile appearance in keeping with its fairy tale image.

About forty kilometres from Jaipur is a four hundred year old Palace—Samode—which belongs to the Rawals—once owing allegiance to the House of Amber. The palace has now been converted into a hotel where the tourists can experience being a Maharaja for the duration of their stay.

As you approach the haveli from Jaipur you pass through the typical desert landscape dotted with *kikar* trees. The village of Samode is small with stone-paved roads—one of which winds up through the rugged hills towards the arched gateway of the palace.

Once inside you are amidst splendour and colour. The walls of the palace are covered with frescoes of floral, paisley and geometric motifs. The Sultan Mahal and Durbar Hall are exquisitely decorated. The Sheesh Mahal, an integral part of any palace is embedded with thousands of polished pieces of mirror. The living rooms are graciously furnished and very comfortable. The glamour is added by the young Rawal Sahib mingling with the guests.

Special musical evenings are organized where folk musicians and dancers enthrall the guests, late into the night. A visit to Samode is essential for anyone who wants to experience living like a Maharaja.

Top: Built atop the Aravalli hills, the Amber Fort afforded protection from the enemy. Climb up the rugged hill upon elephant-back in royal style.
Middle: The Kachwahas created luxurious palaces and gardens within the Amber Fort in contrast to the bleak desert landscape outside the fort walls.
Above: The Rajasthanis specialized in frescoes especially on the theme of Radha and Krishna.

Royal traditions

Rajasthan is the land of monarchs and princes, and glory and splendour. The palaces and forts and the numerous legends give it an aura of wild romance. It is a land of valiant knights in shining armour and beautiful princesses in purdah; of family feuds and internecine warfare; of women who immolated themselves on their husband's pyres; of the brave and chivalrous Rajputs who lived and died with pride, dignity and honour. A land of riches and royal tradition, of pomp and ceremony.

The royal traditions are very much alive today, albeit tinged with Mughal and British influence. The Rajputs through their courage, bravery and fierce loyalty won the favour of the Mughals, and wielded great influence at the Mughal court, commanding their armies and fighting their battles. Through matrimonial alliances they were connected directly to the throne. But as the power of the Mughals declined so did the influence of the Rajputs.

Under the British, they were stripped of their actual powers and became monarchs in name only. However, with the rise of the new elite, the Maharajas acquired a new glamour. They retained their magnificent lifestyles, they travelled extensively, studied abroad, built modern residences, played polo and cricket with the British and squandered their great wealth on a spectacle of kingship.

The Jaipur royal family, the richest and the most influential of all, continues to retain its glamour and mystique. They still live at the Chandra Mahal Palace, the seven-storeyed structure within the City Palace.

After India became independent and the royal kingdoms were absorbed into the Indian Union, Jaipur was declared the capital of the new state called Rajasthan, but the royal family retained its right to the Chandra Mahal and the vast treasury of the House of Amber.

The present Maharaja—Bhawani Singh is very well loved by his people and regularly participates in the festivities in Jaipur. However, the glamour of the royal house of Jaipur, as we know it today, is to be credited to Maharaja Man Singh II and Maharani Gayatri Devi (also known as Jai and Ayesha). This royal couple was the toast of high society in British India as well as in Britain. He hunted and played polo with the British and she was declared one of the most beautiful women in the world.

They lived away from the city, in the Ram Bagh Palace. Once a hunting lodge, it was converted into a fairy tale palace in true royal style with marble fountains, designer drawing rooms, sepia tinted photographs, trophies of polo matches, formal gardens, tennis and squash courts, indoor swimming pool and art deco interiors. The British touch was unmistakable.

This romantic palace has been converted into a hotel where the tourist can live like royalty. There are other residences of the royal family of Jaipur, equally splendid which are now managed by large hotel chains to offer visitors the royal experience. The Raj Mahal Palace, the Jai Mahal Palace, the Ramgarh hunting lodge all offer the palace experience.

Many of the nobility of Rajasthan who owed their loyalties to the House of Amber had magnificent mansions in Jaipur apart from their fort palaces in the desert. Some of these have also been renovated and converted into hotels under the auspices of Heritage Hotels with the help of the government.

The Samode haveli is one such imposing haveli, with large court yards and pleasing interiors. The main Samode palace is forty kilometres out of Jaipur.

An enchanting experience is a stay at the Bissau House in the old city. The approach through congested roads leads to a charming haveli owned by the royal family from Bissau.

The Thakur of Kanota runs a charming hotel in Jaipur called the Narain Niwas, another very interesting place to experience the lifestyle of the Maharajas.

Run in collaboration by the government and the royal owners, these extraordinary Heritage Hotels or royal palaces give you an opportunity to not only live like a Maharaja but perhaps to meet, mingle and dine with a real life royal.

Centre: Glamour personified: Maharani Gayatri Devi—rated by Vogue as one of the ten most beautiful women in the world.
Facing page: The present Maharaja—Bhawani Singh makes a public appearance in one of the royal halls at the City Palace.
Page 70: Rawal Raghavendra Singh of Samode. **Page 71:** Thakur Sahib of Kanota who runs the successful hotel of Narain Niwas in Jaipur.

Pageantry & Plenty

Delhi, Agra and Jaipur offer far more than just historical relics and impressive sights. The three cities are pulsating with cultural life and traditional arts and crafts. For the ardent shopper or souvenir hunter, the bazaars are crammed with a wide and colourful variety of items to choose from. For those seeking cultural entertainment, the winter months are ideal for a visit to northern India. Both the festivals, fairs as well as cultural events (theatre, music, dance performances) take place in the 'season' from October to March. For the gourmet seeking to experience the cuisine of India, the choice is enormous. With prices ranging from the budget to the very steep, you can have your choice of eatables-Indian, South Indian, Chinese, Continental, Thai, Japanese or just plain and simple fast food. Take your pick!

Delhi: Cosmopolitan Glitter

Eating out in Delhi is an electrifying experience. Combine it with an evening's entertainment and you have an unforgettable night out on town. Discotheques, film shows, theatre, dances, music programmes—you can have your choice in Delhi. Winters are a particularly good time for cultural programmes. Mandi House is an ideal venue for classical Indian music or dance performance and theatre. Discotheques are located mostly in the five star hotels and are open to the residents and members.

While shopping or sight-seeing you can make interesting eating halts exploring some of the many restaurants around the city. If you are in Connaught Place you have a wide choice of restaurants as well as cuisines. For Indian cuisine you can try out *El Arab, Abo Dana, Amber, The Host*. If Chinese is your choice, try out *Zen* or *Berco's*, both located in the inner circle of Connaught Place. *Kovil* serves delicious South Indian dishes. A popular restaurant is *Nirula's Potpourri* which has an exotic salad bar. *Nirula's* also has two fast food (hamburgers and pizzas) outlets in Connaught place. *Wimpy's* also has an outlet in Connaught Place, selling fast food.

If you are headed towards old Delhi make a stop at *Chor Bizarre* on Asaf Ali Road where the decor as well as the menu is outlandish and extremely interesting. For true Mughlai cuisine try out *Karim's* in Jama Masjid—the ambience and the flavours are truly oriental. If you are in old Delhi you should spend an evening in the Red Fort grounds watching the sound and light show which brings alive Delhi's Mughal and British past.

Chandni Chowk in the same area has the Bird Hospital, housed within a Jain temple. Hundreds of birds are treated everyday for heat stroke, exhaustion, broken limbs, colds, coughs and fever. The pavements are crowded with astrologers, quacks, faith healers, those who heal with the power of precious and semiprecious stones, or those who sell you digestive tablets and powders as a cure-all.

South Delhi has several restaurants that offer Indian and Chinese cuisine. One of the most popular eating houses which is always crowded is *Sagar* which serves traditional South Indian food. Close to it are the Indian and Chinese restaurants of *Moets*. Quite close to Nizamuddin's shrine is another outlet of *Karim's* serving the royal delicacies of the Mughals. South Extension's *Daitchi* and *Princess Garden* serve Chinese food. Other Chinese restaurants in Delhi are *Fujiya*, *Golden Dragon* and *Lotus Pond*. Indian food is served at *Mini Mahal*, *Sagar Ratna*, *Dasaprakash* and *Coconut Grove*. *Al Kauser* is a small shack located in the Diplomatic Enclave which serves the most exquisite kebabs.

A kilometre away is the Asian games complex next to the Siri Fort Auditorium which has four restaurants. *Chopsticks* is for Chinese, *Ankur* for Indian, *American Pie* for Continental and *Angeethi* for Tandoori Indian food. The Hauz Khas village which has become a major tourist attraction has several restaurants. *Duke's Place* which serves Italian and French cuisine also has a live jazz band in attendance on weekends. *The Bistro* village complex has four restaurants—*Mohalla* and *Khas Bagh* for Indian food, *the Great Wall of the Village* for Chinese, and *Dakshin* for South Indian food. Eating here can be combined with an evening watching folk dance performances against the backdrop of the historic Hauz Khas ruins.

The five star hotels each have several restaurants. Though the prices are a little steep, the cuisine is impeccable. *The Maurya Sheraton* leads in its eating outlets with the *Bukhara*—one of the most famous restaurants in Delhi and *Dum Pukht* which serves a truly royal cuisine. *Bali Hi* on the rooftop serves Chinese food and has a live band and a dance floor. The coffee shop, *the Pavilion*, serves a different cuisine everyday. At *Claridges* you can eat at *Corbett's*—an outdoor restaurant which has recreated the ambience of a jungle. *Dhaba* (Indian) and *Jade Garden* (Chinese) are the other restaurants.

Other Chinese restaurants at five star hotels are *The House of Ming* (Taj Mansingh), *Pearls* (Hyatt), *Taipan* (The Oberoi), *Noble House* (Holiday Inn), *Golden Phoenix* (Le Meridien), *Tea House of the August Moon* (Taj Palace) and *Jewel of the East* at the Ashoka. Thai food is available at *Ban Thai* (Oberoi), and *The Silk Orchid* (Holiday Inn). Japanese food is available at *Tokyo* at the Ashoka Hotel.

Indian food restaurants are *Baluchi* (Holiday Inn), *Kandahar* (The Oberoi), *Pakwan* (Le Meridien), *Dilli ka Aangan* (Hyatt), *Haveli* (Taj

Mansingh), *Handi* (Taj Palace), and *Darbar and Frontier* at the Ashoka Hotel.

French and Continental cuisine is also available in the following restaurants of the five star hotels—*La Rochelle* at The Oberoi, *Pierre* and *Le Belvedere* at Le Meridien, *Captain's Cabin* and *Casa Medici* at the Taj Mansingh and the *Orient Express* at the Taj Palace.

All five star hotels have bars which are open late into the night and coffee shops open 24 hours.

Colour, pageantry and exuberance mark the several **fairs and festivals** that take place through the year in India. Festivity and feasting go hand in hand with religious fervour. Most of the festivals are connected with India's numerous religions and are celebrated with joyous abandon.

Northern India, which burns under the scorching summer sun, re-awakens with the arrival of the monsoons and the subsequent winter months.

Dussehra and Divali are the two most important festivals. Dussehra marks the victory of good over evil as the demon Ravana is defeated in a long drawn-out battle by Lord Rama. People rejoice as evil looking effigies of Ravana and his family are set on fire.

As Lord Rama is welcomed home from exile and his victory over Ravana, people decorate their homes with candles and lights, distribute sweets and the sky is thick with smoke from the firecrackers. It is also a time to worship Lakshmi, the Goddess of Wealth—with merry-making and gambling. Both these festivals take place in October-November.

A variation of *Dussehra* is *Durga Puja*. Though mainly celebrated in West Bengal, several Pujas take place in Delhi. All night cultural programmes and feasting mark the annual visit of the Goddess Durga to crush all evil from the earth.

Just as the city recovers from the *Durga puja* revelry, it is time for *Christmas and New Year*. As all over the world, *Christmas and New Year* bring cheer and joy, presents and parties and feasting on pies and pudding. *New Year's eve* is for the revellers. Connaught Place has a large congregation of people ushering in the *New Year*, but the best way to approach the area is on foot. All the five-star hotels have *New Year's eve* parties featuring international class entertainment and lavish feasts.

The Muslim festivals of *Id-ul-Zuha and Id-ul-Fitr* are celebrated, though the time varies every year as they follow the lunar calendar. Jama Masjid, India's largest mosque is the meeting place for fervent prayers and exchange of *Id* greetings.

Every March northern India witnesses the festival of colours. As winter gives way to spring, it is time to have a splash. *Holi* is the most colourful festival with people smearing each other with coloured powders and throwing coloured water. It is a riotous festival indeed!

India is a treasure house of handicrafts for the **shopper**. Strong and alive craft traditions passed down through the generations, present us with a wealth of attractive items of utility and decoration.

Different regions of the country specialize in different crafts depending upon the ethnic and cultural heritage of the region. Most of these tribal and ethnic riches are available in Delhi. Baba Kharak Singh Marg in Connaught Place has the state emporia which showcase the handicraft traditions of the different states.

Rich and colourful embroidery from Gujarat; exquisite weaves from Madhya Pradesh; stonework, pottery, ceramics and marble inlay from Uttar Pradesh; sculpture in ivory and sandalwood from Karnataka and Kerala; cane and bamboo craftsmanship from the north eastern states of Assam and Tripura can all be bought here.

The best place for handicrafts is the Cottage Industries Emporium on Janpath. On display and sale are a variety of crafts all under one roof. Miniature paintings, embroidery, paintings on wood, cloth and paper, textiles—silk and cotton woven and spun—saris and shawls and even readymade clothes for men, women and children. Leather bags, shoes, wallets, Indian brassware, wood carvings, silver, papier mache, pottery and ceramics, carpets and *dhurries* in wool and cotton, hand knotted or loomspun, furniture, furnishings and even antiques (less than 100 years old) are all exquisitely displayed and sold at fixed prices. Just outside is Janpath, Delhi's bargain bazaar selling souvenirs, books, brassware, leather, papier mache and more importantly garments. Most of the latest European and American fashion garments which are sold at Macy's and Harrods at exorbitant prices can be bought here at a fraction of the price. A side lane has several stalls selling embroidery from Gujarat. Pick up a bargain after hectic haggling. The stately corridors of Connaught Place have luxurious up-market shops for clothes, shoes, sports goods, handicrafts, leather etc. The prices are fixed and rather steep.

There are several other shopping centres in Delhi where an avid shopper can get a bargain for a handicraft or an antique. High flying fashion designer Bina Ramani has a boutique in the ruins of Mehrauli, and yet another boutique in Hauz Khas village. *Fab India* in Greater Kailash I, N Block Market sells readymade cotton outfits in pastel shapes and ethnic designs. *The Santushti Complex* near Ashoka Hotel sells interesting curios, silks, leather bags, pottery and other knick-knacks.

Agra: Medieval Splendour

At Agra, the Mughals patronized the arts and crafts and brought them to a level of perfection. During the reign of Akbar, thousands of traders and artisans were attracted by the riches of the land and came to seek their fortune. The generosity of the emperors and their inclination for the arts allowed the craftsmen to flower.

Even today Agra is famous for the crafts introduced by the Mughal emperors. The opulent and extravagant life-style led to the introduction of carpets with intricate floral motifs of Persian origin. Agra specializes in carpets made of silk mixed with woollen yarn. The carpets get a sheen but at the same time are not as durable as woollen carpets.

Miniature painting was also introduced by the Mughal rulers. The Persian styles were combined with Indian ones to form an Indo-Persian school which in turn influenced the Rajasthani and Himachali (Pahari) schools of art. Most of the books of the time were illustrated with miniature art.

Agra is mostly famous for its marble inlay work which embellishes the Taj and the Itmad-ud-Daulah tombs. Precious and semiprecious stones are inlaid into hard white Makrana marble to make table tops, trinket boxes and replicas of the Taj Mahal.

Agra is also a major leather manufacturing centre. Footwear, garments and bags are made to suit the international market trends. Some of the places to shop in Agra are *Kashmir Palace, Indian Handicrafts, Mughal Marbles and U. P. Handicrafts Palace.*

Within a few kilometers distance from Agra are several places of interest which a tourist may like to visit.

Bharatpur, fifty-five kilometers from Agra is famous for the Keoladeo Ghana National Park, the world's largest wild-fowling centre. Once the hunting preserve of the Maharaja of Bharatpur and his friends, it is today a protected area where the migratory birds return year after year to breed or to escape from the severe winters of Siberia.

Painted storks, spoonbills, cormorants, egrets, herons and ibis fight for living space. Winter brings the shovellers, wagtails, pintails, teal, flamingoes and several other varieties of birds and ducks. The most famous visitor, though rarely seen in recent years is the Siberian Crane. The best season to visit is from September to late March, and the best way to explore the park is on a bicycle which you can easily hire at the park gates.

Just fifty-eight kilometers from Agra is **Mathura**, the land of Krishna. This holy town is mentioned both in history and mythology. Today the only visible link with Krishna is an abundance of cows in the town where Lord Krishna spent his childhood as a cowherd. Krishna's birthplace is marked by a temple where beautiful pictures of Krishna's birth and childhood are illustrated on the walls. Souvenir shops outside the temple sell idols of Krishna.

Mathura is also the centre of the ISKCON, the International Society for Krishna Consciousness which has members all through the world. The ISKCON has built a beautiful complex dedicated to Lord Krishna where devotees sing *bhajans* (hymns) in all languages.

A few kilometres away is **Vrindavan** where Krishna lived with his adopted parents and frolicked with the milkmaids, especially his consort Radha. The temples here are all beautiful and the reverence they command is awesome.

Mathura was also a great Buddhist centre. It was here that the first Buddha images were produced. At the museum in Mathura you can see a large Bodhisattva which belongs to the second century B.C. In fact there existed a Mathura school of art, which was influenced by Buddhism and Jainism.

Jaipur: Treasure-house of Crafts

When Sawai Jai Singh II founded the city of Jaipur, he wanted to make it a leading commercial centre. He invited craftsmen and traders from all over the country to settle in Jaipur. He allotted different sections of the city to different categories of craftsmen. Goldsmiths, jewellers, traders, financiers, dyers, lacquer workers, marble workers all had their own quarters. Even today the bazaars and lanes are named after the craft which you can see being practised. Jauhari Bazaar has the gold and silversmiths at work and the showrooms of all the famous jewellery houses.

Jaipur is a treasure-house of handicrafts, textiles, antiques, jewellery, semiprecious stones, marble statues, wood carving, pottery and emeralds. The city is one of the leading export centres for handicrafts.

Minakari or enamel work on silver is a speciality of Jaipur. Enamelling with or without studded gems is done on curios, jewellery, jewellery boxes, penstands etc. The delicate patterns of birds and flowers are fired in red, green, blue and white; the gold jewel is then given further sparkle with emeralds, rubies and white sapphires.

Jaipur is also the home of printed textiles—handblock prints as well as tie and dye. *Bandhini* and *lahariya* are the tie and dyed fabrics where the fabric is tied into minute knots to form artistic designs and dipped into dye. The cloth under the knots does not take the dye. Lahariya is a pattern of diagonal lines—straight, zigzag or criss-crossed to form geometric patterns. Thirty-two kilometres from Jaipur is Bagru—famous for handblock printed fabrics. Vegetable dyes are used to give the fabric a rich natural colour. The patterns used have been passed down the generations and the colours used traditionally are red and black.

Jaipur is also famous for soft quilts, or quilted jackets, embroidered *jootis*, blue pottery, ivory carving, brassware, copper and marble statues. To buy handicrafts and jewellery some of the shops are: *Rajasthan Government Handicrafts Emporium, Bhandari Jewellers, Gem Palace, Jewels and Art Emporium and P. M. Allah Buksh* (on Mirza Ismail Road). Other areas to shop in are *Adinath* at *Rambagh Palace,*

Mangalam Arts at *Amber Palace, Rajasthan Fabrics and Arts* at *Laxmandwara City Palace, Anokhi* on Yudhishtar Marg and *Silver & Art Palace* on Amber Road.

Rajasthan is a land of **festivals** and joyous gaiety. Except for the summer months when the sun blazes upon the parched land, all seasons have a series of fairs and festivals. Jaipur is famous for three festivals—*Teej, Gangaur* and the *Elephant Festival.*

The arrival of the monsoon brings cheer to the people. Women rejoice by singing and dancing in the rain and putting up rope swings in the gardens. This is the festival of *Teej* held in *July-August*—one of the state festivals of the princely state of Jaipur. Women dress up in their finery, wearing new *lahariya* clothes and colourful lac and glass bangles. The markets wear a festive look and fabric and sweet shops do brisk business. It was on this day that Goddess Parvati was reunited with Lord Shiva after a penance of 100 years. Women seek their blessings for continued marital bliss. The image of *Teej Mata* is taken out in a procession bedecked in a new dress and traditional jewellery. The idol is first worshipped in the City Palace by royal women and then placed on a palanquin to be taken out in a procession through the city as thousands of spectators gather to watch.

Gangaur is essentially a spring festival celebrated all over Rajasthan but with especial vigour in Jaipur. Spring is when Goddess Parvati—also known as Gaur—visits her parents' home and wishes upon her friends everlasting marital bliss. The festival begins on the day after *Holi* in March and continues for eighteen days. On the last day she is given a ceremonial send-off by her family and friends.

Every year on the day after *Holi* in March the old stadium in Jaipur—the *Chaughan* is the venue for a jumbo jamboree. The elephants are magnificently decorated and adorned by their loving mahouts, and then taken out in a procession. They then participate in races, competitions and even beauty pageants.

A recent addition to the festivities is Elephant polo played with long sticks and a plastic football.

The game of **polo** originated in ancient Persia more than 4000 years ago. It moved through Central Asia and to India with the Mughals. But it soon lost its original popularity. It was rediscovered by the British and the Indian royalty who took to the game enthusiastically. Jaipur had one of the best stables of polo ponies and one of the best polo teams in India. Sawai Man Singh, the last Maharajah of Jaipur had over 200 ponies of his own.

The city still is one of the polo playing centres in India and hosts a polo trophy—the Jaipur Cup every year. The polo playing season in Jaipur is from September to March.

© **Lustre Press Pvt. Ltd. 1995**
4, Ansari Road, Daryaganj
New Delhi-110002, INDIA
Phones: (011) 646 0886/ 646 0887 Fax: (011) 646 7185

Text Editor: Rachna Joshi
Design: Sarita Verma Mathur
Typesetting: Fleming George P., Monika Raj Malik

ISBN: 81-7437-008-0

Printed and bound at Singapore

Photocredits
Cover: Pramod Kapoor
Backcover & Title page: Karoki Lewis

Other Photographs by
Ashok Dilwali, Dheeraj Paul, Amit Pasricha,
D.N.Dube, Ganesh Saili, Subhash Bhargava.

Cover: A dancer at the Samode haveli—about forty kilometres from Jaipur where the tourist can experience royal splendour.
The 400 year old haveli belongs to the Rawals who owed their allegiance to the House of Amber.
Title page: Elephants are caparisoned and decorated and well taken care of by their mahouts since they are used as beasts of burden as well as for ceremonial purposes. In fact, in March every year Jaipur holds an Elephant Festival where the elephants take part in sports competitions and beauty pageants.
Half Title page (from left to right): The Qutb Minar built by Qutub-ud-din Aibak in the early thirteenth century stands towering over the ruins of the early kingdoms of Delhi.
The Taj Mahal is clearly reflected in the canal that leads upto it from the main gateway—a view of the Taj as every visitor sees it.
The Hawa Mahal—the concrete curtain built in 1799 by Sawai Pratap Singh, allowed the royal women to observe the festivities and processions in the streets below, without being seen.
Back Cover: Washermen on the banks of the Yamuna with the Taj Mahal in the background.